ANTONIA NOVELLO

Fantastic Physician

Jill C. Wheeler

ABDO Publishing Company

visit us at
www.abdopublishing.com

Published by ABDO Publishing Company, PO Box 398166, Minneapolis, MN 55439. Copyright © 2013 by Abdo Consulting Group, Inc. International copyrights reserved in all countries. No part of this book may be reproduced in any form without written permission from the publisher. The Checkerboard Library™ is a trademark and logo of ABDO Publishing Company.

Printed in the United States of America, North Mankato, Minnesota.
052012
092012

 PRINTED ON RECYCLED PAPER

Cover Photos: Getty Images; Glow Images
Interior Photos: Alamy p. 13; AP Images pp. 9, 11, 21, 23, 25; Corbis p. 5;
    Getty Images pp. 15, 16–17, 19, 27; iStockphoto pp. 6–7

Series Coordinator: BreAnn Rumsch
Editors: Megan M. Gunderson, BreAnn Rumsch
Art Direction: Neil Klinepier

Library of Congress Cataloging-in-Publication Data

Wheeler, Jill C., 1964-
  Antonia Novello : fantastic physician / Jill C. Wheeler.
      p. cm. -- (Women in science)
  Audience: 8-12
  Includes index.
  ISBN 978-1-61783-448-6
  1. Novello, Antonia C.--Juvenile literature. 2. Women physicians--United States--Biography-
-Juvenile literature. 3. Physicians--United States--Biography--Juvenile literature. I. Title.
  R154.N82W44 2013
  610.82--dc23
  [B]
                                    2012011513

CONTENTS

ANTONIA NOVELLO

In 1990, Antonia Novello became the first woman to serve as US surgeon general. She was also the first Hispanic to hold this office.

Novello's journey began on an island in the Caribbean Sea. Along the way, she faced serious health problems and the loss of her father.

But with her mother's support, Novello worked hard to get a good education. She then became a doctor so she could help others.

Novello's work in public health has helped many. She treated sick children and helped those needing **organ** transplants. She worked to limit tobacco use. She also worked against **domestic violence**.

Novello's hard work helped her find her American dream. Today, her story is an inspiration to many.

"Service is the rent you pay for living, and that service is what sets you apart."

— *Antonia Novello*

ISLAND CHILDHOOD

Antonia Coello was born on August 23, 1944, in Fajardo, Puerto Rico. Fajardo is about 30 miles (48 km) southeast of the capital city of San Juan. Antonia was the first child of Antonio Coello and Ana Delia Flores. She had one younger brother.

Puerto Rico is a US commonwealth. And, Puerto Ricans have US citizenship. Those that live in the United States may take part in US government.

Antonia was born with a serious health condition. Her intestines lacked healthy nerve cells. So, they did not work properly. Antonia lived with pain. And each summer, she spent two weeks in the hospital.

Doctors could correct Antonia's problem. However, they needed to wait until she was eight years old. But the year Antonia turned eight, her father died. Her mother had to work to support the family.

The hospital that could operate on Antonia was in San Juan. The long journey was difficult to fit into Ana's schedule.

In addition, Antonia's doctor left the hospital to take a government job. As a result, she would live with pain for ten more years.

OPENING DOORS

Antonia's mother taught math and science. As a teacher, Ana knew the value of a good education. She also knew it meant hard work. Ana would not let Antonia's illness stand in the way. She encouraged her daughter to do her best in school.

Many times, Antonia worked harder simply because her mother expected more from her. But Antonia enjoyed learning new things. She became a very good student.

Ana even changed jobs to be with Antonia as she advanced in school. She was the principal at both Antonia's junior high and high school. She always helped Antonia with her studies. And, she made sure Antonia always had the best teachers.

Antonia found much success in her life. She is thankful that her mother never let her give up as a child.

THE BEST MEDICINE

>> *As a girl, Antonia was a member of the Girl Scouts. She is one of more than 50 million women to have joined this club.*

Even with her mother's help, life was not easy for Antonia. Her illness was tough to deal with as a teenager. She often had a swollen belly.

But, Antonia did not want the other kids to feel sorry for her. So, she joined many school activities. She also used her sense of humor to make friends.

Antonia was in pain. But she laughed a lot and was fun to be around. For her, laughter really was the best medicine!

Through her school years, Antonia stayed focused and positive. In the end, she graduated from high school early. She was just 15 years old!

Antonia's mother (left) watched her become US surgeon general in 1990.

MEDICAL SCHOOL

After high school, Antonia began college at the University of Puerto Rico in Río Piedras. Then at 18 years old, Antonia finally had surgery.

Unfortunately, the operation did not go well. Antonia ended up missing several months of school. But, she did not stay off course for long!

Antonia graduated in 1965. The next year, she traveled to the United States for a second operation. This time, it worked.

Antonia's illness had tested her. But it also helped her decide to become a doctor. She wanted to help others avoid the kind of pain she had grown up with.

Antonia hoped to attend the University of Puerto Rico Medical School in San Juan. At that time, there were few female doctors. And the school only took 65 people per class.

Yet, Antonia was accepted! She worked hard and graduated in 1970. Antonia was finally a doctor.

Antonia graduated from the University of Puerto Rico Medical School in the top five percent of her class.

AGAINST THE ODDS

During medical school, Novello had met Dr. Joseph R. Novello. He was a US Navy doctor working in Puerto Rico. They quickly fell in love.

Following their marriage in 1970, the couple moved to the United States. Novello began her **residency** at the University of Michigan Medical Center in Ann Arbor. She focused on **pediatrics**.

At the hospital, there were few women residents. And, Novello was often the only Hispanic woman around. But she did not give up against these odds.

Novello helped care for many children with kidney diseases. She later became a kidney specialist. She was known for her gentle way of caring for her patients.

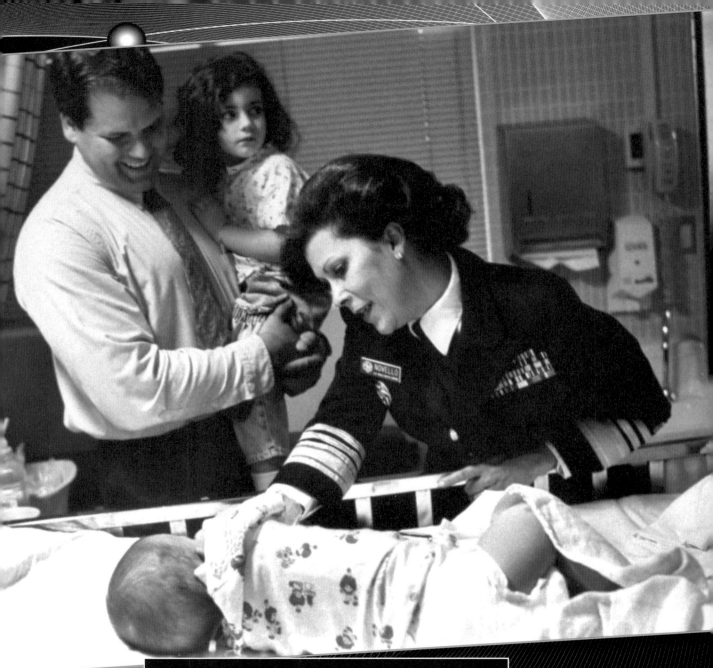

Novello learned much from her young patients in Michigan. Children's health has remained her focus throughout her career.

15

In 1973, the Novellos moved to Washington DC. There, Novello served a **fellowship** in **nephrology** at Georgetown University Hospital. In 1976, she began working at a private practice for children in nearby Springfield, Virginia.

After several years, Novello realized that this work was not enough. She wanted to change laws to improve health care for children and adults.

So in 1978, Novello joined the US Public Health Service (USPHS) Commissioned Corps. Her first job with the USPHS was at the National Institutes of Health (NIH) in Bethesda, Maryland.

Novello also went back to school to study public health. In 1982, she graduated from Johns Hopkins University in Baltimore, Maryland.

Novello and her husband (center) *both followed careers aimed at helping children.*

A Call to Public Service

>> *Thanks to Novello, tobacco companies must now include warning labels on their products.*

Over the next 12 years, Novello rose at the NIH. She began as a project officer. During this time, her reputation grew. In 1983, Novello was awarded the Public Health Service Commendation Medal.

Novello continued to work hard. Together with Senator Orrin Hatch, she helped write the National Transplant Act of 1984. This law was created to help match **organ** donors with patients.

Novello also focused on children with **AIDS**. She spoke out often on this topic. Her efforts helped raise funds to help children with AIDS.

In 1986, Novello was named deputy director of the National Institute of Child Health and Human Development.

In this role, she set national health goals for children. Three years later, she was awarded the Surgeon General's Exemplary Service Medal.

Novello cares deeply for all children. She often makes time for visiting those in the hospital.

US Surgeon General

>> *To date, only three women have served as US surgeon general.*

By 1989, **AIDS** had become a global health concern. President George H.W. Bush and his staff were aware of this. That year, they were also looking for a new US surgeon general.

Novello's special interest in helping children with AIDS caught their attention. President Bush believed she was the right person for the job.

At first, Novello questioned why she had been nominated. She remembered the times she had been the only woman and the only Hispanic in a group. She did not want to be chosen for being different. She wanted the job because she was qualified.

The secretary of health told Novello she was chosen for her skills and work in public service. Congress agreed and approved the nomination.

On March 9, 1990, Novello was sworn in as the nation's fourteenth surgeon general. She became the first female and first Hispanic to serve in this position. Novello was now in charge of protecting the health and safety of all Americans.

Novello thanked President Bush for "bringing West Side Story to the West Wing."

NEW CAUSES

In her new role, Novello continued her work helping children. She fought underage alcohol and tobacco use. She faulted tobacco companies for their efforts to attract young people to smoking.

As a result, Congress passed new laws that helped limit access to tobacco. People could not buy these products without first proving their age.

Novello also brought to light **domestic violence** as a public health issue. Thanks to her, doctors began working more closely with legal and social support groups. The goal was to help people facing abuse at home.

Hispanics also gained from Novello's help. The National Hispanic/Latino Health Initiative was formed. It addressed health issues that affected this community.

Novello made sure her advice was clear enough to help people.

In addition to these efforts, Novello did not forget about **AIDS**. She brought to light the problem of mothers passing **HIV** to their babies. And, she continued to focus on programs that taught others about children with AIDS.

IMPROVING LIVES

>> *The NYSDOH is the largest public health agency in the country.*

In 1992, Americans elected a new president. Bill Clinton took office in January 1993. In June, Novello was ready to move on. During her three-year term, she had addressed the health concerns of young people, women, and **minorities**.

Novello continued to serve others outside of the government. That same year, she joined the United Nations International Children's Emergency Fund (UNICEF). Novello traveled the world to address children's health and nutrition issues.

In 1996, Novello returned to Johns Hopkins University. She served as a visiting professor of health policy and management.

Then in 1999, Novello returned to government work. She was named commissioner of the New York State Department of Health (NYSDOH). In this role, Novello worked to better state health care programs for children, the elderly, and the poor.

Novello served in the NYSDOH from 1999 until 2007.

DR. NOVELLO

AN AMERICAN DREAM

In 2008, Novello joined Florida Hospital in Orlando, Florida. There, she focused her work on women's and children's health.

The following year, New York State officials began an investigation. They said Novello used state resources for personal use while at the NYSDOH. Eventually, Novello pleaded guilty to making a false statement in an official document.

As a result, the court ordered Novello to repay money to the state and pay a fine. She also performed community service in a health clinic.

Today, Antonia Novello continues to serve the public through her work at Florida Hospital. In addition, she gives speeches that she hopes encourage others to do great things with their lives. Novello also hopes that her story inspires them to believe in their own American dreams.

Novello feels honored to serve as a role model for Puerto Ricans and Americans.

TIMELINE

1944	1965	1970	1978	1982
Antonia Coello was born on August 23 in Fajardo, Puerto Rico.	Antonia graduated from the University of Puerto Rico in Río Piedras.	Antonia graduated from the University of Puerto Rico Medical School at San Juan; she married Joseph R. Novello and moved to the US.	Novello joined the US Public Health Service.	Novello graduated from Johns Hopkins University in Baltimore, Maryland.

1986	1990	1993	1999	2008
Novello was named deputy director of the National Institute of Child Health and Human Development.	Novello became the first woman and the first Hispanic to serve as US surgeon general.	Novello began working with the United Nations International Children's Emergency Fund.	Novello was named commissioner of the New York State Department of Health.	Novello joined Florida Hospital in Orlando, Florida.

DIG DEEPER

To become a children's doctor, Dr. Antonia Novello learned many things about the human body. Test your knowledge about our bodies! And get more tips for keeping yours healthy at www.letsmove.gov.

QUIZ:

1 Is someone always reminding you to drink your milk? This is good advice because your bones are busy growing! Some fuse over time, so adult bodies have fewer bones than children do. True or False: An adult skeleton has 206 bones.

2 Feeding your body well is a key part of growing up healthy. According to www.letsmove.gov, which of the following is NOT good advice for good nutrition?

   a. Kids should eat five fruits and vegetables each day.

   b. Portion sizes for kids should be the same sizes as they are for adults.

   c. Kids and adults should drink water instead of fruit juices, soda, and other sweetened beverages.

3 You probably know that a game of hoops is healthier for your heart and muscles than a video game session. But do you know how much exercise your body really needs? True or False: Children need about 30 minutes of activity every other day.

ANSWERS:

1. **True.** Babies start out with about 300 bones! But as kids grow, calcium helps some grow hard and others grow together.

2. **B.** Kids are smaller than adults and should eat smaller portions. A portion size is about the size of a fist — a kid's fist for a kid and an adult's fist for an adult.

3. **False.** As recommended by Michelle Obama's Let's Move! campaign, children need a total of 60 minutes of activity every day. Talk with your family about ways you can get more exercise to stay healthy.

GLOSSARY

AIDS – acquired immunodeficiency syndrome. A disease that weakens the immune system. It is caused by the human immunodeficiency virus (HIV).

domestic violence – an act between members of a family or household which results in serious physical or emotional harm.

fellowship – the position of a person appointed for advanced study or research.

HIV – human immunodeficiency virus. A virus that weakens the immune system and causes AIDS.

minority – a racial, religious, or political group that differs from a larger group in a population.

nephrology (nih-FRAH-luh-jee) – a branch of medicine that deals with the kidneys.

organ – a part of an animal or a plant composed of several kinds of tissues. An organ performs a specific function. Organs of an animal include the heart, the brain, and the eyes.

pediatrics – a branch of medicine that deals with the care of children.

residency – a period of advanced medical training for a doctor after graduating from medical school. A doctor doing this is called a resident.

WEB SITES

To learn more about Antonia Novello, visit ABDO Publishing Company online. Web sites about Antonia Novello are featured on our Book Links page. These links are routinely monitored and updated to provide the most current information available.

www.abdopublishing.com

INDEX